RED SPEEDO

BY LUCAS HNATH

★

★

DRAMATISTS
PLAY SERVICE
INC.

SPECIAL NOTE

Anyone receiving permission to produce RED SPEEDO is required to give credit to the Author as sole and exclusive Author of the Play on the title page of all programs distributed in connection with performances of the Play and in all instances in which the title of the Play appears, including printed or digital materials for advertising, publicizing or otherwise exploiting the Play and/or a production thereof. Please see your production license for font size and typeface requirements.

Be advised that there may be additional credits required in all programs and promotional material. Such language will be listed under the "Additional Billing" section of production licenses. It is the licensee's responsibility to ensure any and all required billing is included in the requisite places, per the terms of the license.

SPECIAL NOTE ON SONGS AND RECORDINGS

Dramatists Play Service, Inc. neither holds the rights to nor grants permission to use any songs or recordings mentioned in the Play. Permission for performances of copyrighted songs, arrangements or recordings mentioned in this Play is not included in our license agreement. The permission of the copyright owner(s) must be obtained for any such use. For any songs and/or recordings mentioned in the Play, other songs, arrangements, or recordings may be substituted provided permission from the copyright owner(s) of such songs, arrangements or recordings is obtained; or songs, arrangements or recordings in the public domain may be substituted.

RED SPEEDO had its New York premiere at New York Theatre Workshop (Jim Nicola, Artistic Director; Jeremy Blocker, Managing Director), opening on March 3, 2016. It was directed by Lileana Blain-Cruz. The scenic design was by Riccardo Hernandez, the costume design was by Montana Blanco, the lighting design was by Yi Zhao, the sound design was by Matt Tierney, the fight direction was by Thomas Schall, and the stage manager was Terri K. Kohler. The cast was as follows:

RAY .... Alex Breaux
PETER .... Lucas Caleb Rooney
COACH .... Peter Jay Fernandez
LYDIA .... Zoë Winters

RED SPEEDO was originally produced by the Studio Theatre (David Muse, Artistic Director; Keith Alan Baker, Managing Director), Washington, D.C. in September 2013. It was directed by Lila Neugebauer. The set design was by Mimi Lien, the lighting design was by Dan Covey, the costumes were by Meghan Raham, the sound design was by Christopher Baine, the fight direction was by Rob Hunter, the dramaturg was Adrien-Alice Hansel, and the production stage manager was T. Scott Wooten. The cast was as follows:

RAY .... Frank Boyd
PETER .... Thomas Jay Ryan
COACH .... Harry A. Winter
LYDIA .... Laura C. Harris

SPECIAL THANKS

To the actors: Haskell King, Marianna McClellan, David Ross, Paul Niebanck, Guy Boyd, Davy Raphaely, Thomas Jay Ryan, Frank Boyd, Laura C. Harris, Harry Winter, Alex Breaux, Peter Jay Fernandez, Lucas Caleb Rooney, Zoë Winters.

To the directors: Linsay Firman, Lila Neugebauer, James MacDonald, Lileana Blain-Cruz.

To the dramaturgs: Adrien-Alice Hansel, Aaron Malkin.

To the theaters: Sara Garonzik, Philadelphia Theatre Company; David Muse, Studio Theatre; Jim Nicola and Linda Chapman, New York Theatre Workshop.

And also: New Dramatists, Jason Padgett, Val Day, Thomas Schall, and Caryl Churchill.

CHARACTERS

RAY—male, late 20s, any ethnicity

PETER—male, late 30s, any ethnicity (same as Ray)

LYDIA—female, 30s, any ethnicity

COACH—male, 50s, any ethnicity

SETTING

In a natatorium.
Present, more or less.
One month before the summer Olympics.

A NOTE ABOUT THE POOL

The setting of the play is a natatorium with the edge of the stage representing the edge of the pool. Different productions have handled this design challenge differently. In the New York production, New York Theatre Workshop built an enormous tank with a clear plexiglass front so that you could see into the pool. It was roughly the width and length of a single lane, and it allowed our lead actor to make his entrance from inside the pool. A prior production at Theatre Exile in Philadelphia made something simpler—essentially a trough at the edge of the stage. It created the illusion of a pool and was deep enough that during the play's final fight, Ray could plunge Peter's head fully underwater.

However, the world premiere of the play at Studio Theatre featured no pool at all, only the suggestion that the edge of the stage was the edge of the pool. But no water.

All options are viable.

What the pool accomplishes, in addition to giving the production an element of spectacle, is that it allows the climatic fight of the play to go to a very dangerous place with an attempted drowning.

In a production that does not build a pool (or at minimum a trough filled with water), an alternate approach to the play's climatic fight is necessary as it would feel a bit silly to have Ray attempt to drown Peter without any water. For that reason, I've included at the end of the script an alternate description of a fight that does not use a pool.

SCRIPT GRAMMAR

Ellipses
A beat. A brief moment to think, to process; sometimes shared, passing back and forth between two or more characters, perhaps a stand-off, perhaps traded glances.

Line Break
Such as:

> RAY.
> I know you're right I fucked up
>
> but but but
>
> like you were talking about

This space between lines implies a breath. Otherwise, where there is no "breath," move through the lines without air.

Dash
If I had no worries about readers being able to make sense of the play on a first read, I'd have written a line such as:

> It's a sacrifice—like a monk, like a—he's a—this is it all he has all he can do tried to work in the outside world, but that was a—he has no skills—He can't function, can't function because he devoted everything to

as:

> It's a sacrifice like a monk, like a he's a this is it all he has all he can do tried to work in the outside world, but that was a he has no skills He can't function, can't function because he devoted everything to

In other words, the dash has no breath, no break. Run it through.

Other Considerations
Fluidity is important. There are many sections of this play that consist of a dialogue of sentence fragments. These lines want to connect seamlessly, no air in between. Doesn't necessarily mean that it's speed-read. But it must be fluid, not staccato.

There's something simply un-American about this. This is about values, about culture, it's about who we define ourselves to be.

—Joe Biden,
on the topic of performance enhancement drugs

Anything you want, you got it.
Anything you need, you got it.
Anything at all, you got it.
Baby.

—Roy Orbison

RED SPEEDO

The set: It's an indoor swimming pool at a gym. Everything is tiled. Everything has that watery blue glow that indoor pools have. The edge of the stage is the edge of pool, and there is water there.

And maybe we can smell chlorine.

Enter Ray: a swimmer. He wears a red Speedo. For the entire play, he only ever wears a Speedo.

Also, he has a tattoo—a big one. The tattoo is of a sea serpent. It begins on his back; it covers almost his entire back. And then the tail of the serpent runs down his backside and wraps around his left leg. It's ridiculous; it's permanent.

And enter Coach and Peter.

And a loud air horn sounds—the sound that sounds when a race starts.

Scene 1

(Ray eats from a bag of baby carrots.)
(Peter speaks to Coach on behalf of Ray.)

PETER.
A man. This man—Here is a man who is nothing short of amazing.
He has devoted his entire life to swimming.
At age 4 he took his first swimming lesson,
age 8 he won his first swim competition,
age 10 he won his first national swim competition,
years pass he's working his way up the ladder,
trying to make it to the Olympics,
and yeah, there was a year or so where he spent time roaming the desert in a van, he was on a

RAY.
spiritual quest

PETER.
took some time and space for himself,
meditated on life and its what-have-you,
but then he came back
and in the years since then he has
consistently worked hard to—skyrocketing, through the ranks—you,
Coach, there for the entire journey, helping him hone his skills—and,
Ray, excelling under your—and the sacrifices he's made—

Here is a man who once got into a car accident, no fault of his own,
a truck slammed into the side of his vehicle, broke two of his ribs.
Ambulance takes him to the hospital,
doctors bandage him, bind up his body, reset the ribs,
all the while, didn't even take any anesthetic,
didn't want to poison his body with—and he should've been at home,
he should've been resting,
but the team had a meet,
and he didn't want to miss it and let you down,
and he took off those bandages and he swam.

And when he launched off the block, his whole torso hit the water
at an incredible—the the the the sheer force with which he hit the
surface of the water, it must have—I can't imagine

RAY.
I have a high tolerance for pain

PETER.
placed first in that race. Had to rush him to a hospital immediately
after—the impact of the water, fractured more bones, broke a third
rib when he hit the—three broken ribs—did for it you, did it for
the club, the team, the—

Here is a man who, in the past 5 months,
twice defeated Michael Phelps in pre-Olympic trials.
Defeated Cullen Jones—I don't remember how many times he—
Once even defeated Ryan Lochte in freestyle, Ray's weakest stroke.

He works so hard.
He practices 6 hours a day in the pool,

does weights for 2 hours,
every day, never misses a practice or meet, right?

he spends so much of his life in the water that his fingers are—the
skin is permanently shriveled, peels off, in chunks

RAY.
's not that bad

PETER.
calcification in his brow-line from the goggles, giving him these
intense migraines that last for days

RAY.
I can put my hand in a flame for up to 32 seconds without flinching

PETER.
… and when he isn't swimming or practicing,
he's teaching children how to swim,
or he's scooping crap out of the kiddie pool,
or he's teaching senior-citizen water aerobics.

Think of everything he has done for this club and your—

And he gives to charity, he cares about animals and their charities,
dog charities and—animals, he—

Women love him. Everyone loves him, but women, *women* love
him the most of—and yes, he does love women back why shouldn't
he—so many women, but what's wrong with

RAY.
they just like me so much

PETER.
he's young and

RAY.
people say I have a lot to offer

PETER.
now he's no scholar

RAY.
nope

PETER.
didn't do well at school, couldn't—devoted all his time to this so
completely devoted his—sure he could've tried to go to college
could've but he put you
and the club
and the team first,
made himself into a swimming machine,
a body that's built for one purpose,
and that means maybe in other areas he's
not so—but this is the sacrifice he's made.
It's a sacrifice—like a monk, like a—he's a—this is it all he has all
he can do tried to work in the outside world, but that was a—he
has no skills—He can't function, can't function because he devoted
everything to

I mean, look at him. You know what I—and yes, I am his brother,
and yes, he is my flesh and blood, my little brother, and yes, I do
care for him, quite a bit.

But I'm not just his brother,
I'm also his lawyer.
And as his legal representative, I am here,
speaking to you the eve before the qualifying trial for the Olympics,
he's destined, he's ready, he will no doubt qualify tomorrow,
his times are—it's not a question. Right?
Correct me if I'm

COACH.
Yes, that is

PETER.
easy, and there you are—he's a swimmer on the Olympic team,
and I have to think that's beneficial, and—this is what every coach
wants, needs for—it's why you do what you do—worked hard,
and Ray's worked hard, and then you get this dipshit-what's-its-
name

RAY.
Tad

PETER.
Tad?

RAY.
Tad

PETER.
his real name—?

RAY.
yeah

PETER.
so we've got this "Tad," who was found with an Igloo cooler full of some sort of performance enhancing whatchamafuckit

COACH.
to be clear

PETER.
yes

COACH.
the cooler was found in the club refrigerator

PETER.
and Ray saw him

RAY.
I didn't

COACH.
he heard

RAY.
I heard from someone that the drugs were Tad's

PETER.
so Ray heard from someone who heard from someone that the drugs are Tad's

COACH.
Ray knows who said, just doesn't want to say

PETER.
for fear of

RAY.
retaliation, someone might punch me in the

PETER.
so with very little evidence, you're going to report this Tad to the swim association

COACH.
Tad is

PETER.
my concern here is not this Tad. My concern is, is Ray. My concern is this gets out, people hear that one of your team's swimmers has been doing performance enhancing drugs, and people start to think that the whole team—you see where I'm going with this— that the whole team is doing—people can't see that Tad's not Ray, that there's no—from the outside, it all looks the same, and then Ray, who's been clean, who's always been clean as a—gets implicated, and then—

Ray's your best swimmer, this Tad—what—third, fourth—whatever, he doesn't count. He's on the team, he wants to swim the qualifying— good for him—he's not gonna make it, try as hard as—not even a contender, not even close to a—the guy doesn't matter unless... *unless* you say anything or make a big deal when you don't have to make a big—because then you draw attention that we don't—then it's this big—
so—I'm asking you
please
don't
bring it up.
Don't stage an intervention.
Don't alert the world anti-doping somethingorother.
Don't tell Tad. Don't remove him from the club, you try to remove him, you don't have much evidence—there isn't even—did you even see him?—he could appeal, ask for a hearing, he asks for a hearing, there's a hearing, this becomes public, and—

I'm going to ask that you do nothing.
Toss the drugs into a toilet and flush 'em an'

COACH.
Peter

PETER.
yeah

COACH.
are you done.

PETER.
… yes

COACH.
because you've been going on pretty non-stop for the past—
> *(Looks at his stopwatch and states the actual length of time Peter's been speechifying.)*

PETER.
go ahead.
I'm done.
I'm—

COACH.
… It is my responsibility to inform the officials, the powers that be, that one of my swimmers has been taking performance enhancing drugs, and it is my responsibility to let them know that Tad's actions may have affected outcomes of prior Olympic qualifying I can see you're gonna try to cut in here and I'm not gonna let that happen Olympic qualifying rounds.
It's an ethical responsibility.

You understand that.
It doesn't matter whether or not anyone finds out,
it's a moral decision that I

PETER.
moral

COACH.
yes

PETER.
how is it

COACH.
morality, integrity, a code of—if I were going to make my decisions
based on whether or not I was gonna get in trouble, or whether or
not someone's gonna find out about it, well then that's not morality,
that's fear, and in our business we don't—

now I'm not gonna have to go to the association if Tad steps up,
if Tad, of his own accord, comes to me and tells me
that he's been doing these drugs, agrees to go ahead and resign,
well, then we have a different

PETER.
that's not gonna

COACH.
I'm optimistic

PETER.
you can't

COACH.
told the team it's come to my attention that there's some doping
going on and

PETER.
so you already

COACH.
if Tad decides to do the right

PETER.
has no reason to

COACH.
's not about that, not about having a reason to

PETER.
how's the club doing?

COACH.
Excuse me—?

PETER.
under your leadership

COACH.
questioning my—?

PETER.
is the club doing well?

COACH.
The club is fine

PETER.
I mean

COACH.
talking about

PETER.
financially

COACH.
we're open

PETER.
and the closings

COACH.
sure we've had

PETER.
looks like you're struggling

COACH.
who hasn't

PETER.
some do and some

COACH.
a lot of

PETER.
cutbacks

COACH.
it's expensive

PETER.
I know

COACH.
what we do

PETER.
what I'm saying is

COACH.
you don't know

PETER.
I know that you're in trouble, and

COACH.
what you know is that if

PETER.
you need Ray, you need him to make it to the Olympics.
He makes it to the Olympics—bring a lot of attention to the club,
name of the place mentioned in every article that mentions Ray,
publicity, you'll be getting calls from every mother in a 100-mile radius,
calling about getting her kid after-school lessons at the club,
type of stuff bring in serious money

COACH.
so

PETER.
I'm

COACH.
saying that

PETER.
I've talked to several

COACH.
have you

PETER.
other coaches

COACH.
who

PETER.
expressed an interest in working with Ray, especially Atlas

COACH.
well now hold on

PETER.
Atlas offered

COACH.
does Ray want that—?

PETER.
I'm just saying

COACH.
Ray, what do you—?

PETER. *(To Ray.)*
don't need to answer the question

COACH. *(To Ray.)*
are you unhappy with—?

PETER. *(To Coach.)*
doesn't have to make any decisions right now

COACH.
never expressed any

PETER.
your actions threaten to hurt his reputation, then I have no choice but to

COACH.
real shitty move

PETER.
detrimental to his

COACH.
what's detrimental is this, this time, this time here, this time we're talking, time that Ray could be preparing, and instead we're talking about

PETER.
concerns

COACH.
more like

PETER.
questions about

COACH.
a threat

PETER.
no

COACH.
yeah you're threatening me

PETER.
I'm just

COACH.
real shitty Peter

PETER.
have so much respect for you

COACH.
you do

PETER.
we're grateful

COACH.
should be

PETER.
all that you've given, let him train here from

COACH.
never charged

PETER.
our family could never afford

COACH.
it's

PETER.
your move. It's up to

COACH.
my

PETER.
decision, you can make a big deal about the Tad situation or—I hate
to do this I really—kills me, I swear, but it's in the interest of—

(To Coach.) and you too, in your interest, I'm

COACH.
I'll do what I need to do

PETER.
yes, you should do what you need to do. I'm just trying to remind
you of what you need

COACH.
I understand, I'll do what I need to do.

PETER.
Okay.
Which is what—?
What is that—?

RAY.
I have an idea

PETER.
you're going to flush the drugs

COACH.
only if Tad comes forward

PETER.
regardless of whether or not

RAY.
I have an idea

PETER.
in the interest of

RAY.
Hey, I have

PETER.
what—?

RAY.
What if Coach didn't flush the drugs,
and what if Coach instead gave you the drugs to

PETER.
what—no

RAY.
didn't even let me

PETER.
go ahead

RAY.
you hold on to the drugs for safe keeping until after the race, and
once Coach has decided what to do after he's had more time to think

PETER.
I don't want them

RAY.
because you're kinda springing this on him, and it's

PETER.
no, I'm not—that's a terrible idea. Sorry buddy, no offense—what
I mean is

COACH.
Peter.

PETER.
Yeah

COACH.
The answer is:
no.

> (Air horn.)
> (Coach exits.)

Scene 2

> (Ray, still eating baby carrots.)

PETER.
first thing we do, day after tomorrow, we move you to Atlas

RAY.
don't really wanna

PETER.
it's best

RAY.
Coach knows me and
PETER.
well

RAY.
you just told him

PETER.
The situation has changed

RAY.
how—?

PETER.
talked to the Speedo people today

RAY.
oh, and

PETER.
they're interested

RAY.
are they going to—?

PETER.
said it was a little unusual to sign someone this early

RAY.
oh

PETER.
I said

RAY.
yeah—?

PETER.
"well that's the point isn't it?"

RAY.
yeah, I mean

PETER.
"you wanna get in on this before Reebok or Nike or Adidas"

RAY.
Nike would be good too, if we had to—not that we

PETER.
told them "you wanna get in on it before there's a bidding war"

RAY.
you said—?

PETER.
to the Speedo people

RAY.
did you talk to Nike—?

PETER.
no

RAY.
but

PETER.
I acted like I—I implied, so that

RAY.
oh

PETER.
said if you're impressed already, it would be stupid not to sign him,
just

RAY.
yeah just do it

PETER.
pull the trigger

RAY.
why not

PETER.
yep

RAY.
cool.
so...

PETER.
So. They said yes.

RAY.
yes

PETER.
you're signed

RAY.
I

PETER.
mean, you have to officially qualify.
That's tomorrow, that'll happen.
When the notarized times get to their office,
you're signed, you're their guy.
And I'm working on *some* exclusivity stuff, so that—you won't be
their only guy, but

RAY.
okay

PETER.
but you're—you know

RAY.
yeah

PETER.
it's

RAY.
cool

PETER.
you're a spokesperson, spokesmodel—whatever you wanna call it

RAY.
and what about

PETER.
as for money

RAY.
did you—?

PETER.
it's a lot of money

RAY.
like

PETER.
I can't say how much

RAY.
oh

PETER.
I mean, it's not a secret—just haven't sorted out the

RAY.
that's okay

PETER.
gonna be a lot of money

RAY.
hey, did you

PETER.
I mean

RAY.
yeah

PETER.
a lot, and that's why we can't have you associated with Tad and his whole—why we have to move you to a different club, different

RAY.
hey did you—?

PETER.
what

RAY.
tell them about my idea

PETER.
who

RAY.
Speedo

PETER.
what idea—?

RAY.
the special edition Speedo that has this part of my tattoo printed on

PETER.
right, *that*

RAY.
comes around like this and up through my

PETER.
deal with that stuff later

RAY.
think people would buy it

PETER.
sure

RAY.
it's unique

PETER.
yep, probably, uh-huh

RAY.
can call it the "Ray Gun"

PETER.
I don't

RAY.
or the "Ray-dar"

PETER.
put it on the to-do list

RAY.
or the "Ray-ger"

PETER.
This deal is very good, you

RAY.
yeah

PETER.
for you

RAY.
yeah

PETER.
and even for me, for us

RAY.
that's good

PETER.
and I'm happy to help out however

RAY.
sure

PETER.
start working with you, and then maybe take on one or two of the others—swimmers I mean—other guys or girls on the Olympic team, I'm sure there's one or two who'd be interested in—help handle their contracts, establish myself as—and who knows, when it's all done—establish a reputation, and take on more clients, bigger clients—I mean you're my star, my priority, don't—but I mean—and I could make the move into athlete management

RAY.
…

PETER.
leave the firm

RAY.
you'd like that

PETER.
well

RAY.
you hate being a lawyer

PETER.
no

RAY.
you hate it

PETER.
just don't like the partners there, and

RAY.
wanting to leave

PETER.
nice to have options—this could become a full-time gig

RAY.
yeah…

PETER.
… What's wrong?

RAY.
Nothing.

PETER.
Are you weirded out by the whole representation thing?

RAY.
What.

PETER.
Me representing you. Me being basically like your sports agent.
Is that okay—?

RAY.
sure

PETER.
mean we never really talked about it. Now's the first it's

RAY.
sure

PETER.
never called myself your representative until back there with Coach.

RAY.
...

PETER.
So. I'm not overstepping am I?

RAY.
nah

PETER.
I mean, I've been doing this work for you, talking to Speedo and
trying to set up a deal

RAY.
thanks
PETER.
takes a lot of time

RAY.
sorry

PETER.
not complaining, and, I mean, just reasonable for me to expect
a cut

RAY.
okay

PETER.
not much, just 10, 15 percent or something,
we can work it out.

RAY.
okay

PETER.
gonna need somebody to do this anyway, and anyone you get will
take a percentage, and I know how you feel about people you don't
know, and so I thought keeping it in the family would

RAY.
okay

PETER.
tell me if it's not

RAY.
It's okay.
I want you to represent me.
I think that's best

PETER.
good

RAY.
wanna baby carrot—?

PETER.
no

RAY.
okay

PETER.
…

RAY.
…

PETER.
so, what is it then—?
what's the

RAY.
what—?

PETER.
matter, something's

RAY.
nothing's

PETER.
something

RAY.
wrong?

PETER.
yeah.

RAY.
… no, I'm

PETER.
thinking—?

RAY.
what if

PETER.
yeah—?

RAY.
… I don't qualify tomorrow.

PETER.
of course you'll

RAY.
but, what

PETER.
no

RAY.
if I don't I'm

PETER.
then

RAY.
nothing happens. Right?

PETER.
well. The deal with Speedo is contingent on

RAY.
me winning

PETER.
but you're going to

RAY.
sure

PETER.
your times haven't dipped

RAY.
no, I know

PETER.
then I don't see

RAY.
but if they did

PETER.
psych yourself out

RAY.
I'm not

PETER.
Don't

RAY.
I'm

PETER.
gonna psych yourself out

RAY.
thinking is all, just

PETER.
next thing I know

RAY.
gonna just

PETER.
go off to the desert

RAY.
nah

PETER.
for two, three years, and

RAY.
just having

PETER.
a panic attack

RAY.
no

PETER.
have a tendency to

RAY.
no

PETER.
that's

RAY.
not what

PETER.
's all in your head

RAY.
Those drugs were my drugs.

PETER.
…

RAY.
…

PETER.
…

RAY.
The drugs

PETER.
what

RAY.
that Coach found

PETER.
Yeah?

RAY.
… The drugs you told him to flush?

PETER.
Yeah.

RAY.
Those were my mine

PETER.
…

RAY.
and I kinda need them

PETER.
need

RAY.
yes

PETER.
how—?

RAY.
to win. Without them, if I don't—I don't win.

PETER.
…

RAY.
why I was trying to get you to take them, you know, when I said

PETER.
yeah

RAY.
and you said

PETER.
yeah

RAY.
wouldn't listen to me—you never—and you—and now he's—and now we're…

PETER.
Those were your drugs.

RAY.
Yes.

PETER.
All of them.

RAY.
Yes

PETER.
those were a lot of

RAY.
s'posed to be enough doses to get me through the next couple of
weeks, to get me through the Olympics, and

PETER.
what about Tad—?

RAY.
Tad—?

PETER.
all of that about Tad was

RAY.
a lie.

PETER.
right.

RAY.
had no choice, it was him or me, and

PETER.
well

RAY.
but it's okay

PETER.
how

RAY.
you said there's no proof

PETER.
so

RAY.
he won't really get in trouble

PETER.
and

RAY.
yeah—?

PETER.
this

RAY.
what

PETER.
… is this a new thing?

RAY.
the

PETER.
drugs, taking them, doping—is it—?

RAY.
No.

PETER.
… How "not new" is this?

RAY.
… I dunno.
Like more than a year "not new."

PETER.
huh

RAY.
Are you upset at me?

PETER.

…

RAY.

I think you're upset

PETER.

no, it's just that—okay—I mean…

RAY.

…

PETER.

I doubt you really need the stuff

RAY.

no

PETER.

you think you

RAY.

definitely need the stuff

PETER.

doesn't make that big a difference

RAY.

definitely makes a

PETER.

so much goes into your performance

RAY.

nope

PETER.

beyond

RAY.

nope

PETER.
what about your, you know, *skills*

RAY.
I have skills

PETER.
yeah, so

RAY.
races are won or lost by fractions of fractions of a second

PETER.
right, so

RAY.
I definitely need the stuff.
I know this.
Really. I do.
I mean, this is like whatdoyacallit—science

PETER.
You don't know anything about science.

RAY.
...

PETER.
...

RAY.
...

PETER.
...

RAY.
... do you wanna know what I know about science?

PETER.
sure why not

RAY.
when they had to make all those cutbacks here

PETER.
yeah

RAY.
and they couldn't afford to have so many
swimmers training for competition,
and during practices I was coming in last, every time,
and Coach was like,
okay, we're gonna have to cut back,
we're cutting back to 4 guys, 4 girls.

And you know, he says to me,
"You and Ron, your numbers are like 4 and 5,"
sometimes I'm like 4 in a race and Ron's like 5

and sometimes I come in like 5 and he's like 4.
and Coach says, "By the end of the year, one of you goes,
and I'm gonna be watching,
so just, you know, know that."

So this is when Lydia and I were together

PETER.
Lydia right okay

RAY.
she's like, "You know, it's out of your control,
it's science, you know"

PETER.
yeah but she was

RAY.
you didn't like her

PETER.
all those sports therapists are

RAY.
I didn't believe her either

PETER.
bad news

RAY.
and I'm like, "No,"
and she's like, "Yeah,"
and she says, "Okay,
don't believe me?
Then look at the fingers."
And I'm like, "Fingers?"
And she's like, "Fingers."
She's like, "The difference between this finger and that finger,
like the length—that's how much testosterone you have,
and how much testosterone you have—that's how fast you swim."
And I'm like, "No,"
and she's like, "Yeah,"
and I'm like okay,
and this is in November, and you know how Thanksgiving takes
place in November

PETER.
yes

RAY.
and you know how Thanksgiving is all turkey-themed and stuff

PETER.
yes

RAY.
and you know how at Thanksgiving they have us make Thanksgiving
dinner for the handicap kids, as like charity,
and they had us do turkeys.
You know, what I'm talking about?

PETER.
No.

RAY.
You know turkeys?

PETER.
I know what turkeys are

RAY.
Yeah

PETER.
but I don't know what you're talking about.

RAY.
you know

(Shows his hand.)

where you make like a turkey like this.
You draw around your hand and

PETER.
Okay. Yeah, I know.

RAY.
and it looks like a turkey thing—finger feathers

PETER.
Yeah

RAY.
each one of the swimmers made a finger turkey for each one of
handicap kids, and I took those pictures and measured the fingers—
used them to figure out and—the two where there was like the less
distance, where they were like closest to the same size,
were me and Ron: we were like the same distance.

PETER.
okay

RAY.
But that's not all: the other guys—here's the order of the other guys—
the order the other guys always came in when we raced were
Tad
then Rob
then Craig.
And the fingers were like that too:
Tad's like the longest and then Rob and then Craig.
So like depending on your finger length, that's it, that's the order
you're gonna win in a race.

46

And I'm like, "No way"
and Lydia is like, "See?"
and I'm like, "No way," that means there's like nothing I can do,
and she's like, "Yeah,"
and I'm like, "That's messed up,"
and I'm like, that really messes with my head,
and I'm like, everything I thought was true is a lie,
and I'm like, I'm like I'm totally screwed,
I'm like totally fucked, cuz there's this *limit*, and no matter what I do,
I can't get past that limit.

And she's like, "Well I think I can get you something that could help,"
she's like "See what happens if you try the stuff,"
and I'm like, "What is this stuff,"
and she's like, "It's all natural,"
she's like, "It's from baby fetuses or something."
And I'm like, "Okay"…

And I tried it.
And it worked.
And I went from being number 4 all the time
to being number 3 all the time,
to being number 2 a lot of the time,
to being number 2 all of the time,
and… then to number 1 most of the time.
And then I beat Phelps, and I beat Cullen, and I beat Lochte,
and that's when the world started to notice me.

PETER.

…

RAY.

…

PETER.

…

RAY.
I know that you're thinking this is wrong,
you think I'm breaking the rules,
but I mean if you read the rules, if you sit down and read them,
I read them, and I really think I have a good case

PETER.
you don't

RAY.
rules say

PETER.
I know

RAY.
yeah—? well what are they—?

PETER.
…

RAY.
number one you can't take the drugs because they hurt you, and these drugs don't hurt me

PETER.
don't know that they don't

RAY.
nah, they don't, I know, I'm fine, I've been fine. Look at me

PETER.
and

RAY.
the number two rule is because they make it unfair

PETER.
right

RAY.
but in my case, they make it fair

PETER.
no

RAY.
we have science evidence for that

PETER.
you're kinda

RAY.
wrong?

PETER.
yes

RAY.
No.
Think about it

PETER.
I am

RAY.
not so different from, what's-it-called with colleges—to help people
get into colleges

PETER.
what?

RAY.
you know, to even things out

PETER.
affirmative action?

RAY.
yeah, it's just like

PETER.
nothing like affirmative action

RAY.
how is what I'm doing not like affirmative action

PETER.
what do you think affirmative action is

RAY.
when you don't have the same advantages as other people so the

government gives you a little extra help

PETER.
no, that's

RAY.
not what it is——?

PETER.
no

RAY.
so what is it——?

PETER.
I don't even know where to begin, it's so

RAY.
not answering the question because you can't

PETER.
one is about race, the other is about physical limitations, there's no

RAY.
exactly the same thing

PETER.
it's really not

RAY.
isn't the color of your skin just physical?
PETER.
Ray.

RAY.
in Buddhism they say

PETER.
Stop.
I'm not questioning whether or not what you're doing is right.
That's not my primary concern right now.

I'm trying to figure out whether or not you're gonna get caught

RAY.
… I'm not

PETER.
because, no, no, listen, my shit is on the line too. I'm associated
with you. I'm working with you. We're not just brothers, we're in
business together, and you do something shady that means looks
like I'm doing something shady, okay? So you if you get caught

RAY.
I haven't

PETER.
so far. But let's not forget, you left like what like 20 plus doses of
the stuff in a refrigerator…
in your coach's office

RAY.
kitchen, everybody uses it, not just coach

PETER.
doesn't make it better.

RAY.
didn't want the stuff to get too warm,
they were in a cooler but they were also in my car trunk,
and it was unseasonably warm

PETER.
That was stupid.

RAY.
I know

PETER.
and that's exactly how you're going to get caught.
But you don't have to be stupid about this, you don't have to

RAY.
That's why I need your help.

PETER.
…

RAY.
cuz of you, coach has my drugs locked up in his office

PETER.
...

RAY.
You said you were my representative, so help me

PETER.
what is it that you need me to do

RAY.
5,000 dollars

PETER.
you mean you need me to give you 5,000

RAY.
yeah

PETER.
for drugs

RAY.
yeah

PETER.
no *way*
the drugs cost that much

RAY.
yeah

PETER.
you're crazy

RAY.
it's late, it's really last minute,
it's probably going to cost more than usual

PETER.
but 5,000

RAY.
and they know I need it, they know it's the night before the final—
so they're gonna totally jack up the price because

PETER.
you know this

RAY.
no yeah I just got off the phone with

PETER.
I really

RAY.
what—?

PETER.
really don't like that Lydia is involved with this

RAY.
but she's

PETER.
don't trust her, don't see why she would want to help you

RAY.
you're the one she hates

PETER.
you're the one she dumped

RAY.
we were gonna get married

PETER.
you're delusional

RAY.
but then you screwed her over

PETER.
I did nothing

RAY.
made her lose her license, and her job

PETER.
it's not like I was her lawyer, I wasn't

RAY.
you knew stuff about her case

PETER.
I knew only what you told me—just gave her some advice

RAY.
and you told the oppositional lawyer stuff about her.

PETER.
I don't think I said that much, nothing that was all that

RAY.
I heard you, I heard it happen, you said

PETER.
She was going to lose regardless.

RAY.
I know but

PETER.
was just saving my colleague some time on the research end,
we all do that, it's normal, I save him some trouble so maybe
someday he'll do the same for me

RAY.
she was the only person
who really understood me,
and it's like you took that away,
and now I have no one now.

PETER.
You're being melodramatic

RAY.
not

PETER.
better off without her,
don't need to be associated
with people like that.

RAY.
… well anyway
you don't have to worry
because
it's not Lydia that I get the stuff from.
Since we broke up, I've been getting it from this guy

PETER.
what guy?

RAY.
His name is Jasper.

PETER.
And who is he—?

RAY.
you know, just some guy
PETER.
the guy who's jacking up the prices last minute

RAY.
why're you asking all of these questions?

PETER.
Because you're asking me to give you 5,000 dollars
to get illegal drugs

RAY.
not illegal, technically

PETER.
from people I don't know,
all of this after I've just set up a deal with a major corporate sponsor.
I can think of a dozen ways this can go wrong.

RAY.
…

PETER.
Type of thing puts my reputation on the line.

RAY.
Mine too.

PETER.
I have a job. I have a high-paying job,
I have a family,
I have a wife,
I have a kid, a two-year-old, a daughter
and soon my daughter's going to be going to school
and she's not going to a free school, she's going to an expensive school,
because if she doesn't go to the expensive school, then she's already I
mean, you know the future it's gonna be rough with where America
is and the future

RAY.
we didn't have money

PETER.
we were lucky. We're doing better than we should. But the fact is:
people with money are better than the people without money.

People with money are better schooled,
better fed, better trained, better cultured.
They're the people who go to museums and opera and the theatre,
and, you know,
they take their kids there, and the kids get this
culture and shit and it makes them smarter.
And rich parents they aren't stressed out—maybe a little, I guess,
distant, big deal. Poor parents—our parents—those parents—those
are the kinds of—knock around their kids, can't feed them or let
them get fat on McDonald's—don't care if they do their home-
work—It's not their fault poor parents suck, because trying so hard
to survive makes you meaner, shittier—you're just trying to—

rich kids have it so much easier than we did. They get better treatment
from everyone else in the—9 times out of 10—You take a poor kid, a
poor kid who has talent, has to put up with all the shit of being poor
and has to work harder because of it—a rich kid with the same talent
doesn't have to put up with so much, and that kid'll still go farther
than the—and I don't want my daughter to suffer, or not be as—

because I fucked up, put her in a position where she has less.

That's what I have to lose, that's what's at—And what do you have
to lose?
What?

RAY.
lots

PETER.
No. You don't.
You have nothing to lose because
you don't actually have anything.
No wife, no kids, no house.
You have no skills—other than that you can swim—okay
but you have no actual

RAY.
I know

PETER.
you have

RAY.
nothing, and nowhere to go,
and no real job, and sometimes I live in my car,
and sometimes I don't have a car and live in people's basements,
or I sleep in the locker room, and I don't tell you about it because
I don't want to have to keep asking you and mom for—
and I don't have an education or a degree,
and no future, and I'm getting too old,
and this is it. This is it. My one shot.

PETER.
...

RAY.
but...
I win,
you win,
and if I win big,
you win big,
you win bigger than you've—you can—the stuff you could do for your

daughter and your—I mean—and what do you do for it what are you risking, I mean, really, come on, dude. And don't I deserve a chance, and don't I—Don't I deserve—isn't that the American thing—?

PETER.
dream—?

RAY.
everyone gets a—just loan me the money, just—come on, do it. Do it. Loan me the money or I'll kill you I'll bash in your skull nah I'm just kidding come on just help me out dude. Just help me out. Really.

> *(Air horn.)*
> *(Exit Peter.)*

Scene 3

> *(It's late at night, at the pool. The lights are mostly off, the room is lit by the light coming from the pool—that watery blue glowing light that pools emit in the dark.)*
> *(No one's around, except for Ray and Lydia. Ray at the edge of the pool, legs hanging off into the water.)*
> *(Ray's still eating baby carrots.)*

LYDIA.
I used to date this guy, long before you

RAY.
that's cool

LYDIA.
he's now in the movie business,
and he's like really high up I mean you look him up online you'd see he's really big

RAY.
wow

LYDIA.
and so I call him up and tell him what happened.
about you know, my "situation"

RAY.
yeah

LYDIA.
because, I don't know, I had just gotten to thinking about all the
stuff that had gone down with the case, the hearing, the—and
thinking to myself what's the point of bad things happening if you
can't turn them into something good,

and so I tell the movie producer—my ex—I tell him my story—
about how I have this true story about me
and a friend who was really sick
and about how she needed a certain medication in order to live
but she couldn't afford it,
and so I used my unique connections in the pharmaceutical trade,
risked my career and my life (in a way)
to obtain this medicine for this dying friend,
and I did it, and I saved her, but then the government found out,
and I got arrested, and the rest of—you know if we made it a movie—
the rest of the movie could be
about my court case and how I got railroaded
and the struggle
and the way the system is just the way it is
but I fight it anyway

RAY.
wow yeah

LYDIA.
and there are a lot of parts where it could be a like a thriller
like that other movie about that other woman, it won all those awards

RAY.
am I in this movie—?

LYDIA.
I'm changing all the names

RAY.
so that means—?

LYDIA.
don't want your brother suing me for something like defamation of

character

RAY.
is he the bad guy in the movie

LYDIA.
I dunno Ray what do you think, is he a bad guy—?

RAY.
sounds like a movie that could make a lot of money

LYDIA.
I dunno it'll probably take a while not like I've signed anything yet or
just talking about it
with people—but I

RAY.
really sounds like you're doing great,
I'm really happy that you're

LYDIA.
I mean the whole sports therapy thing—
that's all gone because, well, you know—I lost my license,

but I mean there are a lot of things
that I can apply for license or no license,
some stuff in offices or even retail,
I mean I really don't care,
I just need some money is all:
got rent to pay, bills, regular old living expenses—
I'll waitress, I'll work in a coffee shop—doesn't matter—
but no one's hiring me
no one's even calling me in for an interview
or they might call to schedule an interview
but then they end up canceling—
called the lawyer who had worked on my case,
asked him, what's up with this,
an' he's like, "well your former employer can't say
negative things about you,
but when employers call them
they can just say 'no comment,'"
and "no comment" means that's
just as bad as saying what did happen

RAY.
right

LYDIA.
and then some job applications,
they ask if you've ever been arrested,

and I just don't think that's right, I mean come on,
anybody can be arrested for anything,
shouldn't matter, but then
when you say "yes," "yes I was arrested,"
they start asking follow-up questions,
and it all comes out, and none of what comes out
is any good, all looks
really bad.

RAY.
…

LYDIA.
But look at you—you're gonna be a spokesmodel for Speedo

RAY.
yeah

LYDIA.
bet that pays even more money than movies

RAY.
Yeah…

LYDIA.
Why—?

RAY.
I guess because it's hard work keeping real still for photos for
several hours at a time

LYDIA.
no I mean

RAY.
what—?

LYDIA.
why did you call me here?

RAY.
I just

LYDIA.
I'm standing here trying to figure it out—something you're not saying

RAY.
I missed you

LYDIA.
Is that all—? You just

RAY.
missed you.
I miss you Lydia

LYDIA.
all of a sudden—?

RAY.
no, I

LYDIA.
never called

RAY.
you dumped me

LYDIA.
you weren't curious how I was doing?

RAY.
told me to never call you.

LYDIA.
And I see you got a new tattoo

RAY.
it's a sea serpent

(He shows her.)

You like it?

LYDIA.
It's… big

RAY.
his tail even goes down through

LYDIA.
yeah

RAY.
and down to my
just thought it would be good for publicity and stuff,
because we all kinda look the same when we swim,

because we all have goggles and swim caps,
so I thought it would be a good idea
to make myself really easy to spot,
so like when I'm swimming,
and they have the camera overheard watching us swim,
it's really easy to know which one I am,
and everyone will be like "whoa who's that guy with the sea serpent,
he's awesome."
and then I have this idea for a special edition Speedo

LYDIA.
with that

RAY.
has this part of the tail painted on it

LYDIA.
right

RAY.
got it for publicity

LYDIA.
publicity

RAY.
yeah

LYDIA.
not to cover up the old tattoo?

RAY.
nah, that just sorta

LYDIA.
you can still sorta see the L and the Y…

there's the D…

can still kinda make it out.

RAY.
…

> (Now that she mentions it, we can totally make out the name
> "LYDIA" buried within the body of the sea serpent.)

LYDIA.
You don't miss me.
You move on, you get over things,
things wash over you—just slide on by.
And I think that's good—'s healthy.
We've both moved on, and

RAY.
but I haven't moved on. You're all I think about

just think you're so smart,
so tough, and you have such good ideas,
and you're really—with all your court problems,
how you're able to talk to lawyers and police and stuff, and—
I couldn't do that, I would—just totally freak me out—
you, you're just so good at being in the world,
and I'm not so good at being in the world,
and

LYDIA.
I don't want to take care of you

RAY.
no

LYDIA.
that's

RAY.
not what I meant

LYDIA.
it's what you want, I can tell

RAY.
No…

I'll take care of *you*.
I'll take care—I got this deal with Speedo,
all I have to do is make it into the Olympics
and and and get that Speedo deal,
and get that money,
and that will lead to even more money,
money I can live off of—*we* can
live off of for the rest of our—cuz
once people see me at the Olympics,
and you know, I've got my you know

LYDIA.
tattoo—?

RAY.
that and my outrageous and likeable personality,
and people are gonna be like, "wow," and there will be all these offers
to do things that aren't swimming, that are like
being on TV or magazines and interviews, and—
I don't even care if they're really like making fun of me,
cuz if they're paying me, cuz if I have money,
then I can be like a real person
with a house and a car and a bank and a doctor and a dog for a pet
and a—a family, because that's what real people have.
I want to be a real person kind of person, not just a stupid

LYDIA.
…

RAY.
an' it's why I'm doing this, an' it's why I don't just run off,
an' why I don't just do what I did last time,
an' why I don't just steal another van and
run off into the desert and—because
this time this time I have
you to think about
and you to—that's what

LYDIA.
…

RAY.
and you know I've been with a lot of girls since you.
I can get girls easy and—but you're the only one I think about,
and even when I'm with other girls,
I close my eyes, and I think about you

LYDIA.
yeah

RAY.
even when I jerk off, I think about you, you're

LYDIA.
well that's nice to hear

RAY.
all the time

LYDIA.
okay

RAY.
like 15 times a day

LYDIA.
you jerk off 15 times a day—?

RAY.
yeah

LYDIA.
you

RAY.
do it so much I even ripped the penis skin, it's all

LYDIA.
Ray.

RAY.
yeah—?

LYDIA.
you know what that is, right—?

RAY.
love—?

LYDIA.
… no

RAY.
yeah, I think it's

LYDIA.
wait hold on how much *are* you taking—?

RAY.
wha—?

LYDIA.
the stuff

RAY.
dunno what you mean

LYDIA.
the HCG

RAY.
I dunno

LYDIA.
you're taking more, aren't you

RAY.
not really

LYDIA.
like, *a lot* more

RAY.
a little more

LYDIA.
you put so much testosterone in your body
that you're in a constant state of horniness,
that you've gone an torn a hole in your dick does it hurt—?

RAY.
I have a high tolerance for pain

LYDIA.
oh honey you don't want me, it's just chemical, that's all

RAY.
no, I know that's not

LYDIA.
hope you're being careful, hope you're

RAY.
I'm careful

LYDIA.
they keep records, they test you every week, stuff won't show up

RAY.
I know

LYDIA.
but they *do* monitor the levels, okay, and if you

RAY.
I'm careful.

LYDIA.
Who's supplying—?

RAY.
the stuff—?

LYDIA.
yeah

RAY.
Jasper.

LYDIA.
Jasper's in jail

RAY.
I know

LYDIA.
well, if

RAY.
I stocked up.

LYDIA.
You call me the night before the qualifying round

RAY.
no, I

LYDIA.
you put on this act like you miss me,
act like you want to get back together

RAY.
no, really, that's not

LYDIA.
okay, now it makes sense you ran out of the stuff

RAY.
no really

LYDIA.
just so you know

RAY.
it's for you that I need to win, it's so we

LYDIA.
I don't have any.

RAY.
Any what?

LYDIA.
Stuff. I don't—no, when I got in trouble, I got out of that business,
I don't—nope

RAY.
oh

LYDIA.
nothing, so if that's

RAY.
no no it wasn't

LYDIA.
Literally, the only "drugs" I have in my apartment
are three doses of medicine
for my cat.
Who is sick—

RAY.
Colonel Fuzzman—?

LYDIA.
yeah

RAY.
oh how's he doing—?

LYDIA.
he's sick

RAY.
oh yeah

LYDIA.
so yeah

RAY.
…

LYDIA.
…

RAY.
…

LYDIA.
…

RAY.
Okay. Yes. I do need the stuff.
I had the stuff, but the stuff went missing,
and tomorrow, I need the stuff to qualify.

Okay? But it's not like you think.

See, I had this big plan.
I've been trying to figure how,
how am I gonna win you back,
and I knew that it had to be big.
Everything I've been doing
for the past coupla months,
has been about that, making like this big…
thing was gonna like blow your mind.

LYDIA.
Uh-huh.

RAY.
Like this, so picture it:
I was gonna win the Olympics,
and I was gonna be on TV,
and they were gonna put the microphone in front of me,
and I was gonna hold up the medal and say,

71

"This is for Lydia.
Love of my life.
Arrow of my heart."
And then I was gonna take out a ring,
take out the box, open it, and show it to the camera like this,
and I was gonna say, "Lydia, will you marry me."
And this was gonna be on national television,
and they'd put a phone number on the lower part of the screen
for you to call, and I'd stand, with the ring,
and with my medal, and I'd just wait,
the television cameras all watching me,
you at home, watching me, and I'd wait for your call,
and I wouldn't leave, I'd just stay there, and wait,
even if it took for the rest of my life.

LYDIA.
…

RAY.
…

LYDIA.
yeah I don't believe you.

RAY.
I knew you'd say that,
so…

> *(Ray produces a ring.)*

like I said, this wasn't how I planned it,
how I planned it was gonna be much more impressive.

LYDIA.
oh.
Ray.
no.

> *(Ray gets down on one knee.)*

RAY.
I think we should

LYDIA.
don't

RAY.
what

LYDIA.
say it

RAY.
marriage?

LYDIA.
I can't.

RAY.
Why not?

LYDIA.
I'm leaving.

RAY.
What?

LYDIA.
The country.

RAY.
What?

LYDIA.
I'm leaving the country.

RAY.
This one?

LYDIA.
You know because
I owe months of back rent and back taxes.
I can't get a job, I mean sure there's the whole movie thing
but I haven't really talked to those people in I dunno three months—
I mean I don't think it's a bad sign or—I've heard these things take time
and you know, they have my contact info, I'm reachable

but yeah, at the end of the month, I'm gone, I'm leaving the country,
starting a new life with a clean record.

I've already given away all my stuff.
I have nothing except for my cat and a one-way ticket
out of the country.
(*Looking down.*) … actually I was also wondering if
you would take Colonel Fuzzman
because I know how much you two liked each other, and
and I wanted him to be with someone who liked him

RAY.
no

LYDIA.
okay then I'll find someone else

RAY.
no I mean you can't leave.

LYDIA.
I can't stay.

RAY.
Then let me come with you.

LYDIA.
I don't want that.

RAY.
You said—you said I wasn't serious

LYDIA.
yes

RAY.
you said I'm not committed

LYDIA.
right

RAY.
and so—?
Here I am.
Serious. And committed.

And if I can just qualify tomorrow,
I'll have money from Speedo to take care of you,
to pay all of your bills, or or or
if you want to go to another country,
I can do that too, buy you a nice house in Europe or someplace like
Europe.

LYDIA.
Ray
nothing undoes what you did,
nothing undoes the fact that
your brother screwed me over,
and you didn't stand up for me

an' you told me that you overheard your brother
talking to the opposing council about my case

RAY.
I mean I might have—

LYDIA.
I found out that that's not allowed,
that if the judge had known
that your brother had done what he'd done,
the case would've gotten thrown out
and I would've won, and I wouldn't be in the position I'm in

RAY.
no

LYDIA.
yeah

RAY.
naw that doesn't make any sense

LYDIA.
because the hearing has to be fair. The other side isn't allowed to get
information that's been said in confidence.

RAY.
but I mean

LYDIA.
what—?

RAY.
you did was sorta illegal

LYDIA.
is that what you really think—?

RAY.
I just mean that what you did was sort of, on the technicalities, against
the law

LYDIA.
if it's against the law to save my friend's life, then it's the law that's wrong

RAY.
But you barely knew the woman, and and

LYDIA.
and what

RAY.
it's not like you did it for free you charged her for the medicine

LYDIA.
I don't get the stuff for free

RAY.
you charged her for *more* than it cost you

LYDIA.
not much

RAY.
marked it up

LYDIA.
I have to make a living too I'm taking a risk by

RAY.
I wouldn't have charged her.

LYDIA.
Charging her or not, doesn't change the basic situation

RAY.
kinda

LYDIA.
no

RAY.
I'm just saying all I'm tryin' to get at is that
we all do things that are sorta good
and sorta not so good,
you
and me
and even my brother

LYDIA.
honestly Ray,
it's not even about the fact
that your brother did what he did,
it's about you not doing anything,
it's about when you heard Peter talking to the other lawyer,
his buddy, his friend,
talking about me when he had no business sharin' my private shit

you shoulda said,
"Dude that's not cool."
If you just gone to him and said
"Dude, I don't like what you did to my girlfriend."
Even that, even that small miniscule gesture
would have meant so much to me.

Why didn't you do that just that little bit?

RAY.
he doesn't like it when I talk to him about his work stuff

LYDIA.
So?

RAY.
He wouldn't have changed his mind, and—I mean, he was helping

me out at the time.
I had all those credit card debts,
bills from the car wreck and from—all sorts of stuff,
and he was helping me out, and I needed that. I was

LYDIA.
living with me

RAY.
so

LYDIA.
you weren't paying rent, it's not like you weren't also getting
something from me, you

RAY.
didn't have any money, and even now, he's still helping me.
I can't—I mean—I train all day, every day.
This is like a full-time job.
I do this, and then they pay me a little bit of money to lifeguard
during like
the senior-citizen swim hours.

LYDIA.
He was paying your bills

RAY.
person's gotta survive

LYDIA.
and *I* was giving you someplace to live

RAY.
yeah, I know, I was like between a rock and a hard place

LYDIA.
had a nice thing going, and you didn't wanna give it up

RAY.
twisting my words.

LYDIA.
…

RAY.

…

LYDIA.

…

RAY.

… would you just look at the ring?

LYDIA.

… No.

RAY.

… it's a really nice one.

LYDIA.

…

RAY.

expensive

LYDIA.

… yeah.

RAY.

cost me like
… 5,000 dollars

LYDIA.

…

RAY.

…

LYDIA.

…

(Ray puts away the ring.)

RAY.

I know you're right I fucked up

but but but

like you were talking about

like those jobs you're applying to where they won't hire you
because you were arrested, like where
it's totally not fair to have something you did just not go away,
how people should give you a chance to do better
because if you're never given a chance to do better
then nothing will ever get better

don't you want things to get better?

    (Lydia nods.)

I can't undo what happened,
but I can do better.

LYDIA.
…

RAY.
so…

… what if

LYDIA.
…

RAY.
listen, what if—what if the judge knew that the lawyers fucked you
over, what if

LYDIA.
how—I would need

RAY.
a statement—?

LYDIA.
yeah

RAY.
from me. If I wrote up a—what do they call them—?

LYDIA.
affidavit—?

RAY.
if I did one, wrote down everything

LYDIA.
... about your brother—?

RAY.
told the courts that I overheard him tell the other lawyer things he
wasn't supposed to say.

LYDIA.
...

RAY.
If I did that, you could uh you know appeal,
and you could win for sure.
You could get your sports therapy license back,
you could get work—ya know until the movie thing happens,
like you said it might take a long time and until then—
you could clear your name,
and you wouldn't have to leave the country.
Or you could, if you wanted, but either way,
you'd have a clean record.
Come on. You don't wanna leave. You have friends here.
You like it here.
You don't wanna leave Fuzzman,
you don't
And you love being a sports therapist,

hanging out in gyms all day,
giving dudes massages,
it's your favorite.

You get your license back, and I'll talk to some people,
I'll get you a spot working with the Olympic swim team, yeah?

LYDIA.
...

RAY.
You miss me.
You do. I know you do.
I can tell.
I can tell.

LYDIA.
…

RAY.
…

LYDIA.
Your brother could lose his license

RAY.
you lost yours

LYDIA.
could get fired

RAY.
and so did you.
Fair's fair, right—?

LYDIA.
… I guess

RAY.
but

LYDIA.
yeah—?

RAY.
one thing

LYDIA.
what

RAY.
if I do this, then—*really* important I win tomorrow, even more important than before, I need to—for us, and I need you to get me

one more dose of the stuff.

LYDIA.
… I

RAY.
need it for tomorrow

LYDIA.
Ray, I can't—I don't

RAY.
just get it for me

LYDIA.
where—? how—?

RAY.
I know you have ways of getting the stuff.

LYDIA.
really don't. Ray, I really

RAY.
can't take no for an answer.

> *(Air horn.)*
> *(Exit Lydia.)*

Scene 4

> *(After the qualifying race.)*
> *(Just Ray and Coach.)*
> *(Ray is physically depleted.)*

COACH.
a bunch of members of the press.
There's some newspaper or web people,
and some TV people

RAY.
TV cameras—?

COACH.
a couple

RAY.
oh

COACH.
is that a problem—?

RAY.
no

COACH.
just wanna take your picture, probably take our picture together,
then take a couple more of just you

RAY.
okay

COACH.
they'll wanna talk, ask you some questions

RAY.
what kinds of questions?

COACH.
Is there anyone you want to thank—?

RAY.
oh

COACH.
How do you expect to do in the Olympics?
Uh, maybe something like, "You just broke the 100 meter
breaststroke world record,
do you think you'll be able to top that time in July?"

RAY.
okay

COACH.
pretty easy questions for the most part

RAY.
yeah

COACH.
if you get stuck, I'll be there,
but I want you to really make an effort
to field these questions on your own, okay?

RAY.
okay

COACH.
don't be turning to me lookin' for my approval or

RAY.
yeah okay

COACH.
You're an Olympic swimmer now

RAY.
yeah

COACH.
You won. You qualified

RAY.
yeah

COACH.
so be proud, be confident, I know you can do that. I've seen you do
that

RAY.
yeah

COACH.
none of these one-word answers like yeah or okay or

RAY.
okay

COACH.
don't be shy, but also don't be arrogant.
Don't be a jackass up there.
Don't do any trash talking.
Don't—you get what I'm talking about—?

RAY.
yeah I

COACH.
so say they ask you, "Ray, how are you feeling right now?"
What do you say—?

RAY.
good

COACH.
no, you gotta

RAY.
I don't know

COACH.
what do you—?

RAY.
I guess, "I'm feeling a lot of emotionality right now,
lotta strong things inside me all," I dunno

COACH.
... okay, that's a little better you can also just say that you're grateful
for the opportunity to represent your country at the upcoming
summer Olympics. You can say that you're excited to compete on
the American team, and you're a really big fan of the other team
members, and it's an honor

RAY.
yeah I can do that

COACH.
and lastly, no matter what,
don't chalk your success today
up to luck

RAY.
luck?

COACH.
Don't, you know say, "I feel really lucky to be here, to make it on
the Olympic"

RAY.
okay

COACH.
it's a shitty thing to say.
This—what you've done—has nothing to do with luck.
What you've done that's about hard work and discipline, sacrifice.
And to say you feel lucky is a slap in the face
to the swimmers you bested,
and it's a slap in the face to you, and to me.

We worked hard to get here.
… Wouldn't you agree?

RAY.
… yeah.

COACH.
You believe that.

RAY.
… yeah.

COACH.
Do you think you could've done this on your own? Without…
help?

RAY.
… uh

COACH.
do you, Ray—? Did you need any help to get where you are—?

RAY.
no

COACH.
no?

RAY.
I did it on my own

COACH.
you did

RAY.
I think so

COACH.
You sure?

RAY.
(?) … yeah.

COACH.
… so then
what am I doing here—?

RAY.
oh, you

COACH.
had nothing at all to do with—?

RAY.
no yeah, sure, thought you meant like no yeah you've been a big
part of

COACH.
how.

What do you think I've done.

RAY.
You coached me

COACH.
what does that—?

RAY.
gave me advice

COACH.
yes and

RAY.
and you watched me swim.
And you told me what you saw,
and when you saw something wrong, you told me.
And you would sometimes change my stroke, make sort of
adjustments to

COACH.
when I did that, sometimes you would say "no no no,
don't make me change my stroke, that's my—"
remember sayin' that—?

RAY.
yeah

COACH.
give me a real hard time

RAY.
naw I just

COACH.
and gee how'd that turn out for ya

RAY.
it improved

COACH.
what

RAY.
my stroke

COACH.
your performance

RAY.
yeah, that

COACH.
an' look where you are.

RAY.
...

COACH.
So you would agree that we've been a good team,
you agree that I've been instrumental in

RAY.
yeah, sure

COACH.
I think so too.

Which is why I was surprised last night,
when I get a call from Coach Reed—you know Coach Reed over at
Atlas

RAY.
not really

COACH.
he knows you

RAY.
heard his name

COACH.
and certainly knows your brother—told me yesterday that he and
Reed had been talkin', well, I figured sure Peter probably called
Reed and asked around, tried to suss out interest—figured that
much—didn't think that your brother had told Reed that *you*
wanted to leave us—

RAY.
...

COACH.

that you had problems with my coaching style, that you thought I
was a little—word he used was
"abusive"—

RAY.
naw I

COACH.
that you had problems with the changes I was making to your program
and your strokes

RAY.
I swear I

COACH.
thought he should maybe give me a call and give me a heads up,
out of courtesy, because coaches—we don't poach, we don't—that's
not our

RAY.
wasn't me, it was Peter, I didn't

COACH.
so what is a body to do?

RAY.
…

COACH.
Ray—?

RAY.
I dunno what that means

COACH.
lemme tell you, I've seen it happen—happens a lot:
some coach'll be the one who works with an athlete for
7, 10, 15 years even,
and that athlete will grow and develop under the coach,
and they'll form a real bond, and that coach'll know that swimmer's
every instinct, every twitch, every muscle,
and he'll know the swimmer's mind, his habits,
his bad habits, his idiosyncratic—and eventually

that swimmer becomes a star,
and gets all these other folks wantin' to work with him,
and so he leaves his coach of 7, 10, 15 years,
for another coach, at maybe a bigger, better-funded club,
a coach with maybe a little more clout, a little more fame.
But then, the swimmer stops performing, his times drop,
and now he's a huge disappointment.
Everyone's disappointed with the—not the coach—the swimmer.
They say, oh, gee, that guy, he choked, got performance anxiety—
bullshit.
New fancy coach didn't know the swimmer.
Didn't know how to work with him.
Didn't know his body.

I'm not tryin' to scare you.
I just want you to understand
the risk you're about to take unless,
you go to your brother and say, "no."
Tell him, "I wanna stay where I am."
Tell him, "What Coach is doing is working."
Why would you want to mess around with something that works?
Why take the risk?

RAY.
…

COACH.
not luck that got you here.

RAY.
I know.

COACH.
So, you're going to tell your brother

RAY.
I can try

COACH.
wanna go to that Olympics with you—might be my last chance

RAY.
can try, but my brother doesn't always do what I ask him to

92

COACH.
it's your signature that's going to sign on to Atlas, not Peter's

RAY.
I'm just sayin'—he has a way of getting his way

COACH.
tell him no, just don't sign any

RAY.
don't understand, it's all a lot more complicated than

COACH.
complicated how—?

>   *(Peter enters.)*

PETER.
...

COACH.
...

RAY.
...

PETER.
Coach.

COACH.
Peter.

PETER.
congratulations.

COACH.
... thanks

PETER.
must be proud.

COACH.
well he

PETER.
gave quite a

COACH.
yes

PETER.
mind if we—?

COACH.
sure

PETER.
just be a moment.

COACH.
he's supposed to

PETER.
press—?

COACH.
yes

PETER.
no, I know.

COACH.
I'll be back in about 5 minutes, better be ready, Ray.
        (Coach exits.)
PETER.
…

RAY.
…

PETER.
What were you guys talking about—?

RAY.
Atlas

PETER.
he

RAY.
said Reed called him

PETER.
he knows—?

RAY.
Reed told him

PETER.
that's it—?

RAY.
yeah but

PETER.
's fine don't worry about

RAY.
I just

PETER.
hey

      (Peter produces a FedEx envelope.)

catch

      (Tosses it at Ray.)
      (Ray catches it.)

RAY.
What's this—?

PETER.
gift

RAY.
from

PETER.
Speedo

     (Ray opens the package.)
and from me—a gift from—a little pre-signing congratulations token

     (Takes a Speedo from the envelope.)
     (Holds it up.)
     (A dragon tail wraps around the surface of the suit.)
RAY.
awesome

PETER.
I think it looks—but I know you really

RAY.
wanna get like 20 of these

PETER.
yeah well they exist

RAY.
change into this for my press conference

PETER.
sure why not

RAY.
… thanks, that's
nice of you

you're so nice, sometimes, yeah, you're

PETER.
…

RAY. *(Lying down on the ground.)*
… really appreciate

PETER.
you okay—?

RAY.
I

PETER.
what

RAY.
I did something.

PETER.
what did you—?

RAY.
I'm definitely getting the Speedo deal, right?

PETER.
yep

RAY.
and that's gonna make us both of a lot of money

PETER.
I hope so

RAY.
like more money than you got working as a lawyer, right—?

PETER.
maybe, if everything goes well

RAY.
we'll be okay

PETER.
Yes.

RAY.
and you're

PETER.
yeah—?

RAY.
gonna leave your job

PETER.
well

RAY.
You don't have to be a lawyer anymore.

PETER.
No.

RAY.
You don't want to be a lawyer anymore

PETER.
not really but

RAY.
what

PETER.
probably going to gradually phase out my career as a lawyer

RAY.
When?

PETER.
don't know, sooner than later.

RAY.
But you don't need it anymore, we've got the Speedo deal.
Why not quit now?

PETER.
I will. I've got things to finish up

RAY.
should quit as soon as possible

PETER.
cases pending, I'd be leaving people in a pretty bad spot if I left now

RAY.
but if you need to leave

PETER.
why are you asking—?

RAY.
I dunno.
No reason.

PETER.
What

RAY.
nothing

PETER.
there's something

RAY.
no.

PETER.
There's definitely something—tell me

RAY.
you know how I said I was gonna get the drugs from that guy Jasper

PETER.
Yeah?

RAY.
Yeah well he's in jail, so I couldn't go to him

PETER.
...okay

RAY.
so instead I went to Lydia

PETER.
ah.

RAY.
really didn't have a choice, so you know

PETER.
go on

RAY.
and at first Lydia was really mad,
and she didn't want to sell me the stuff.

PETER.
Okay.

RAY.
She was still really pissed off at me about well a whole bunch of
things, but

PETER.
got it.

RAY.
She wouldn't take the money.
She wanted something else.

PETER.
…

RAY.
wanted me to sign something.
She wanted me to sign something that
said you spoke with the other side, other lawyers,
that you broke the court rules,
and the lawyer rules
by talking to the other side.

PETER.
…

RAY.
She really had me up against a wall didn't have a choice, I mean

PETER.
so she's

RAY.
going to appeal,
and she's going to tell the judge,
and she's going to tell the people who give out lawyer-licenses.

PETER.
...

RAY.
...

PETER.
Oh.

RAY.
...

PETER.
Well...

RAY.
...

PETER.
...

RAY.
...

PETER.
...

RAY.
what are you thinking?

PETER.
...

RAY.
what are you thinking, Pete?

PETER.
...

RAY.
… what are you—?

PETER.
For starters

RAY.
…

PETER.
it will take the courts a long time to do anything about this.
These things, they take time

RAY.
okay

PETER.
secondly—you said she's appealing this—?

RAY.
yeah

PETER.
won't do any good

RAY.
why not

PETER.
she broke the law

RAY.
she said

PETER.
yes, it'll get her case reopened

RAY.
but

PETER.
it's not as if the affidavit changes the the the merits of the

RAY.
are you

PETER.
sure—?

RAY.
Yeah…

PETER.
Yeah. I'm sure.

RAY.
and will it—?

PETER.
what

RAY.
you know, with your job, will it—?

PETER.
get me fired—?
or disbarred—?

RAY.
…

PETER.
it might, yes—I guess… yes. But that's fine—that doesn't—it's fine.
I'm moving on from all of that—we're gonna, start this new thing,
and it's okay. It's great.

RAY.
you sure—?

PETER.
yeah

RAY.
So you're not…
you don't feel like I

PETER.
like you what—?

RAY.
I dunno

PETER.
betrayed me? fucked me over? threw me under the train?

RAY.
… yeah

PETER.
… nah

RAY.
…

PETER.
… I think

RAY.
…

PETER.
it's like how on airplanes, when you fly how they say if the plane is
crashing they tell you *if* the plane crashes, you should put on your
own oxygen mask first, and then help the person next to you, because
if you don't put on your own mask, you don't save yourself, you die
and then you're useless to anybody else. Right?

RAY.
okay

PETER.
You did the only thing you could,
and the only thing you should.
When you go for what you want,
when you think about yourself,
when you do what's best for you,
everyone benefits

RAY.
yeah I guess

PETER.
if you hadn't done it, would either of us have gotten what we wanted?
Would you have won the race?

RAY.
No.

PETER.
Right. And then the Speedo deal wouldn't have happened,
and I'd be stuck at the firm for the foreseeable future, miserable.
You—you'd be even worse, you'd have nothing

RAY.
yeah

PETER.
so

RAY.
okay

PETER.
…

RAY.
…

PETER.
…why don't you go get yourself put together for the

RAY.
okay

PETER.
… Ray—?

RAY.
yeah, I'll

PETER.
… you gotta get up, buddy…

> *(Ray tries to stand, weakly.)*
> *(He wobbles.)*
> *(He doubles over.)*
> *(He vomits water—orange water.)*

RAY.
…

PETER.
…

RAY.
…

PETER.
…

RAY.
…

PETER.
what was that—?

RAY.
I'm okay

PETER.
Ray don't—Sit down. Sit.

RAY.
okay

PETER.
maybe you shouldn't do that press thing

RAY.
no

PETER.
people don't want to watch you throw up

RAY.
do you think I need to go to the hospital?

PETER.
… no.

RAY.
you know how it feels when you have food poisoning

PETER.
yeah

RAY.
that's how I feel right now

PETER.
oh well, so you've had food poisoning and made it out fine, so you probably

 (Coach enters.)

COACH.
…

PETER.
…

RAY.
…

PETER.
hey Coach

COACH.
…

PETER.
Ray's gonna skip that little press conference, if you don't mind.

COACH.
…

RAY.
…

COACH.
… He okay—?

PETER.
yeah, he's

COACH.
Ray—?

RAY.
yeah—?

COACH.
you okay, buddy—?

RAY.
I'm okay

COACH.
…

RAY.
…

COACH.
cuz you're layin' face-down on the ground

RAY.
the ground feels good on my face

COACH.
he looks sick

PETER.
nope

COACH.
get up, Ray

PETER.
Coach—?

COACH.
…what.

PETER.
leave 'im alone.

COACH.
…

PETER.
…

COACH.
Ray, I want to see you stand

PETER.
Ray, don't stand.

COACH.
… Ray—?

PETER.
don't

COACH.
…

RAY.
…

COACH.
taking his pulse

PETER.
Coach, I'm asking you kindly
to respect our
         (*Coach ignores Peter, takes Ray's wrist.*)
Don't violate my client.

COACH.
…

         (*Ray groans.*)

We need a doctor

PETER.
we don't

COACH.
he's going to the hospital

PETER.
Ray do you want to go to the hospital—?

RAY.
no

PETER.
Ray, show Coach you're fine

COACH.
no

PETER.
show Coach you can stand up

RAY.
okay

COACH.
Ray

> *(Ray stumbles to his feet.)*
> *(He is wobbly.)*

RAY.
see—?

PETER.
see. He's great

> *(Ray falls to the ground.)*

RAY.
I wanna go to the hospital.

COACH.
calling the ambulance

PETER.
5,000 dollars

COACH.
what—?

PETER.
5,000 dollars just to walk away, leave us

COACH.
he

PETER.
doesn't want to go to the hospital, he doesn't want to see a doctor, you're

COACH.
bullshit

PETER.
no

COACH.
Ray did you take anything—?

PETER.
don't answer

COACH.
did you—?

PETER.
doesn't have to answer the question

COACH.
Jesus Peter, what if he's really

PETER.
no

COACH.
he's *sick*.

PETER.
… 10,000 dollars. Walk away

COACH.
he's your brother

PETER.
I'll take care of him, 10,000 dollars

COACH.
Ray, what did you take—?

RAY.
nothing

COACH.
when I call 9-1-1
I need to tell them what you took, what did you

RAY.
HCG

PETER.
15,000, Coach, I'll pay

COACH.
HCG—?

PETER. *(Taking out his wallet, taking out cash.)*
Look I have about 400 right here

COACH.
HCG doesn't do that to you

RAY.
's what I normally take

PETER.
just take the money

RAY.
been taking it for—year, two years

PETER.
Ray, stop talking

COACH.
where is it—?

RAY.
wha—?

COACH.
the stuff

PETER.
there's no stuff

RAY.
my duffel bag

> (Coach grabs the duffel bag before Peter can get his hands on it.)
> (Coach opens the duffel bag.)
> (He takes out a vial, looks it over.)

PETER.
20,000 to walk away, don't call the ambulance, no doctors, forget
this ever happened...

COACH.
...

PETER.
...

RAY.
...

COACH.
...

RAY.
...

> (Coach is still staring at the vial.)

PETER.
Coach?

COACH. *(Gestures to the vial.)*
… you don't know what this stuff is, do you

PETER.
it's

COACH.
what

PETER.
I mean I

COACH.
The label says metronidazole—Ray, did you read the label before you—?

RAY.
yeah, I guess, I dunno

COACH.
metronidazole is not HCG. It doesn't make you swim fast

RAY.
… oh—
what is it—?

COACH.
metronidazole?

RAY.
dunno what that is

COACH.
cat medicine.

RAY.
…

COACH.
I know.
My ex-wife had a lot of sick cats.

RAY.
…

COACH.
You're not gonna die, Ray

RAY.
that's good

COACH.
just gonna feel really sick

RAY.
okay.

PETER.
…

COACH.
…

PETER.
Coach—?

COACH.
…

PETER.
What are you going to do—?

Coach?

… Coach

… come on, a little,
feedback here

COACH.
…

PETER.
cuz I mean what just happened I'll tell you what just happened:

somehow Ray ingested cat medicine. It upset his stomach.
He had a panic attack. In the middle of this panic attack
he started talking about HCG—what is that some sort of
performance enhancing thing?
I don't know about these types of things. Nor does Ray.
He was panicking at the time, speaking nonsense,
you can't put any weight on that, means nothing.

Okay and so you think you also heard him say
that he's taken HCG in the past,
that this time it was just cat medicine,
but in the past, all those other races, he did take drugs?
You might even be thinking that those drugs that you found the other
day were Ray's. Sure that stuff you found, that definitely wasn't
cat medicine, but it also definitely—I assure you—definitely wasn't
Ray's.

RAY.
no it was mine

PETER.
and there he goes, in a state of I-dunno-what—confusion,
overwhelmed by his life-changing win today—?
winning is hard, it's emotionally hard—
you understand, once Ray signs with Speedo,
he's a corporate entity, he—saying shit about Ray
is tantamount to saying things about
uh, uh international corporation,
and you go and you start making accusations about him,
you hurt their company, you hurt their investment,
you cost them money,
and then they'll come after your ass, their people, their lawyers,
you think you have problems now, you, you're
worried about the club closing, losing your job?
What they'll do to you is worse, a lot worse,
because
because you don't actually have proof.
You *don't* have test results.

You *don't* have anything concrete.
So what, he said something there about having taken HCG. So what.
It's all what you say versus what we say
and you know what we're gonna say.

… I suggest we should just go our way and you go your way, and we don't need to have anything to do with one another

and the money's yours, that money I offered that's a real offer, 20,000 dollars, that's a lot, and you could put it back into the club, you could pay your employees, pay some bills, pay yourself I don't care what you do with it, it's yours.

RAY.
Coach, you should just get rid of me.
I'm no good—just—why don't you

COACH.
Ray

RAY.
I fucked up, I did

COACH.
are you trying to tell me what to do—?

RAY.
…

COACH.
are you trying to tell me what to do—?

RAY.
no

COACH.
sounded like you trying to tell me what to do.
I'm kinda sick of people tryin' to tell me how to run my

RAY.
I

COACH.
's not your job and
        (To Peter.)
not your job

117

RAY.
I broke the rules

COACH.
I'm talking

RAY.
yes sir

COACH.
I think you're tryin' to pussy out of competing,
I think you're scared you're gonna fail—
and I don't respect that, you understand—?

RAY.
no I

COACH.
shut it—what I'm seein' is someone who wants to do what he did x-
number of years ago when he was this close to makin' it, and then
when the heat got too hot ran into the goddamn desert disappointing
every—makin' an ass of himself, total embarrassment, cuz he got
scared, cuz he wanted to go run back to mommy

RAY.
the drugs in the fridge were

COACH.
don't you bullshit me—keep that up an' I will get rid of you faster than

PETER.
absolutely right, Coach. I'm glad to see you taking a

COACH.
drugs were Tad's drugs

PETER.
yep, that's exactly—listen to him

COACH.
I flushed the drugs.
That's the end of that.

We're moving forward

RAY.
but what about

COACH.
you were tempted. I understand.
Today—and only today—you tried
to take something you shouldn't take,
but you ended up *not* taking
what you thought you were taking,
and ended up taking nothing,
an' as far I'm concerned you

RAY.
meant to cheat

COACH.
your performance out there—that was a result
of the work *we've* done—right?
You and I—what we've been working on for years.
That was what that was. Okay?
And that's why I'm not gonna take Peter's deal.

Peter, I'm not gonna let you pay me off
just so you can move Ray to another club,
that's not right, after everything I've invested into Ray and his—would
hurt Ray's performance—in the hands of another coach who doesn't
know him inside out he'll lose. I'm not going to let that happen.

PETER.
…

COACH.
So right now, you're gonna promise me,
that Ray stays where he belongs,
stays with me, under my supervision and guidance,
and together we'll take this to the Olympics,
make damn sure that Ray follows through and performs,
because I know that's what you want
and that's what I want,
and that's, whether he understands it or not, that's what Ray wants.

So do we have a deal—?

RAY.
no

COACH.
sorry, I'm not talking to you, I'm talking to your representative.

RAY.
not just some thing you

COACH.
Peter manages you, not you

PETER.
yes, Coach

COACH.
"yes" what?

PETER.
we have a

> *(Air horn.)*
> *(Coach exits.)*
> *(A little later.)*
> *(Ray, still face on the ground.)*

RAY.
…

PETER.
…

RAY.
…

PETER.
…

RAY.
…

PETER.
...

RAY.
...

PETER.
Ray—?
come on

>   *(Ray rolls over.)*
>   *(Air horn.)*
>   *(Later.)*
>   *(Not much has changed.)*

RAY.
...

PETER.
...

RAY.
...

>   *(Ray gets up and leaves.)*
>   *(Now Peter is alone onstage.)*
>   *(Just standing there.)*
>   *(All by himself.)*
>   *(Thinking.)*
>   *(Contemplating.)*
>   *(Trying to figure out what to—)*
>   *(Air horn.)*

Scene 5

(Still, later.)
(Ray reenters.)
(He's wearing his new Speedo.)
(He's eating from a bag of carrots.)
(There's something ice cold, steely, unusually calm about Ray throughout the scene. In fact, he doesn't look at Peter. Just stares out, stone-faced.)

PETER.
…

RAY.
…

PETER.
…

RAY.
…

PETER.
I actually think this is the best-case scenario

RAY.
…

PETER.
right—?

RAY.
…

PETER.
I mean, you won,
and you won on your own without

RAY.
Not really

PETER.
…

RAY.
just a trick is all

PETER.
what trick

RAY.
Today—this morning I
tricked myself without even knowing it.
Thought I was taking stuff, and so
then my body thought I was taking stuff,
and made my body start producing you know

PETER.
testosterone—?

RAY.
Yep.
It was all psychotic.

PETER.
psychosomatic

RAY.
Yeah, that too

PETER.
…

RAY.
I never swam times like that, never

PETER.
came close

RAY.
nope—don't know how I did what I did,
except that somehow I psyched myself into it—
and now I know I psyched myself,
the problem is if you need to psych yourself
how do you psych yourself
if you know you're psyching yourself—?

… an' the answer is you can't.
And then when I can't do it again in three weeks,
everyone's gonna start asking questions,
an' then

an' then we're all fucked.

Just a matter of time

PETER.
no

RAY.
If I go to the association now I think I can make a deal with them

PETER.
whoa

RAY.
where they suspend me

PETER.
hold on

RAY.
the world anti-doping agency doesn't get involved

PETER.
you're not

RAY.
I'll get them to agree to not investigate,
no more questions,
no hearings,
no one gets in trouble

PETER.
no one will get in trouble. Anyone makes any accusations, I'll

RAY.
rather lose the money than get the money,
and then lose everything and have everyone in the world
see me lose everything—think that would be worse

PETER.
just get you more of the stuff, get back on the stuff
so your times don't change, and

RAY.
you, an' you and Coach, just a bunch of

PETER.
what

RAY.
think I'm—like I'm a thing, just out to

PETER.
thinking about it too much

RAY.
How can I not? How can I not think about it—
How can I not think about all sorts of things,
all sorts of things I know now that I didn't know before,
things you can't unthink.

PETER.
…

RAY.
…

PETER.
…

(Ray turns to face Peter, looks him in the eye.)

RAY.
You were gonna let me die

PETER.
what—?

RAY.
back there, back then

PETER.
…

RAY.
when I was

PETER.
I I was just

RAY.
were gonna let me die,
an' pay Coach to help let me die.
PETER.
… so you're gonna go and turn yourself in and kill your career just
to get back at me because I—what

RAY.
weren't gonna let me go to the hospital

PETER.
you didn't need to go to the hospital

RAY.
maybe I did

PETER.
no, you didn't, you're fine look at you

RAY.
but you didn't know that then

PETER.
no, I

RAY.
couldn't know

PETER.
no, I knew,
I *know* you.
I know how you can get

RAY.
was sick

PETER.
panicking and you

RAY.
felt I was

PETER.
if we went to the hospital and they ran tests and found some sort of
illegal substance in you, well, I mean, you would've definitely regretted
that

RAY.
not if what it was
was killing me

PETER.
I was protecting you

RAY.
from

PETER.
the possibility that someone would find out something that would
destroy your career

RAY.
and then you wouldn't make any money off of me

PETER.
well Ray, I mean, let's be honest: with that affidavit
you did kinda put me in the position where
your well-being and my well-being
and my family's well-being are inextricably—
I mean, not that I'm complaining or anything—I agreed to go in
on this

RAY.
so that makes maybe letting me die okay?
I don't understand.

PETER.
…

RAY.
is that what you're trying to say—? because

PETER.
look I don't know why I'm getting all the blame here.
I haven't heard you mention the person who actually *poisoned* you.
That person seems to be getting off scot-free

RAY.
Lydia didn't

PETER.
go to her, you pay her money, money I gave you by the way,
you make a deal with her
wherein she's essentially getting me disbarred
in exchange for drugs
that are supposed to help you win a race,
and instead she gives you something
that makes you sick.

RAY.
…

PETER.
I mean, that's fucked up, that's a sociopath an' here you are acting
like *I'm* the bad guy

RAY.
but she didn't

PETER.
give you those drugs—?

RAY.
never said she gave them to me.
I *said*
I got them from her.

PETER.
what's the

RAY.
I took them

PETER.
and she

RAY.
told me that she didn't have the drugs.
She told me that she gave up dealing that stuff.
I didn't believe her, thought she was—I dunno—
just didn't wanna get in any more trouble with the law,
and I understand that, and I didn't want—but
things were going "okay" between us, and talking was—
and the more we talked, the more it was like it was
before everything got bad,
and we just sat here,
and then I kissed her,
and then she just held me for a while,
and that was nice, and I knew yeah
I really miss her, and I knew yeah
she really is like I remember her being,
and not at all some bitch you tried to make me think she was

PETER.
I never

RAY.
and I went back to her place

after she fell asleep, I went down to her refrigerator—
that's where she normally keeps stuff,
and I saw some stuff that I thought was—and I took it

PETER.
the cat medicine

RAY.
it was in the same kind of sort of looking bottles they put the—so I

PETER.
that's

RAY.
what happened.

PETER.
…

RAY.
Lydia doesn't want to hurt me.
She actually cares about me, unlike you
who was gonna leave me to die on the floor puking up my guts
begging you to take me to a hospital

and she—and I'm happy,
and I'm thinking maybe she'd,
eventually you know, down the line

maybe kids,
a house,
a car,
a dog

an' I dunno, we can just go
somewhere
far away from here,
and maybe I don't need to be some Olympic swimmer,
and I'll just get a job,
and it'll probably be a shitty job,
and I'll probably suck at it,
and I'll probably get fired,
and I'll just get another shitty job,
and I'll just keep getting fired from shitty jobs,
and I won't care about the fact that I suck at all those jobs,
because I don't need to be that great, I don't—

PETER.
you said—
you said you signed an affidavit in order to get the stuff

RAY.
what—? I said

PETER.
it was the only way you

RAY.
I thought

PETER.
but she didn't give you any drugs

RAY.
I got

PETER.
them because you more or less stole them
or stole what you thought was

RAY.
but

PETER.
so, I'm sorry,
I don't understand
why you wrote up that affidavit.
You told me you had no choice but to—
but it doesn't sound like—
Can you explain that to me?

And the money I lent you, what was that

RAY.
outstanding expenses

PETER.
not why I gave you the money.
So, I'm still confused.
Are you telling me that you just killed my career as a lawyer
for—what

RAY.
the situation was complicated

PETER.
no, that doesn't—did you just throw me under the train
so you could get back together with Lydia—?

RAY.

…

PETER.

…

RAY.

…

PETER.
You have a debt, and you're gonna pay that debt.
You owe me, I own you

RAY.
you don't

PETER.
after all the money I've given you,
all the bills I've paid off,
protecting you, protecting your interests,
watching out for your career,
keeping you out of jail
am I making this up, am I misremembering—tell me, am I—?

RAY.

…

PETER.
wasn't easy to make that car accident look like it wasn't your fault,
wasn't easy to explain away what seemed to look like

RAY.
wasn't my fault

PETER.
any judge with half a brain—wasn't easy to keep
vehicular manslaughter charges off the

RAY.
gonna hold that over my head for the rest of

PETER.
come to me, begging me, telling me you win, I win,

and I figure yeah, I've carried you for a long time now,
it's about time that you, after all I've—
so I'm gonna make you follow through.
This is your burden, you carry it, and you better do a damn good job,
you better do everything in your power to—because if you don't,
if you back out of this Speedo deal,
if you don't perform at the Olympics,
or if you go to the association,
or if anyone finds out about your doping,
then I promise, within 24 hours, police will show up on Lydia's doorstep,
and don't you doubt I can't find a way to make that happen,
don't even try me, you better bet your ass, that—do you understand?

RAY.
…

PETER.
You don't put my life on the line so you can fuck some cunt

RAY.
don't call her that

PETER.
she's a cunt, Ray, she's
        (Ray walks over to Peter.)
don't like when I call her a cunt—?

RAY.
no

PETER.
sorry but she's a
        (Ray hits Peter in the stomach.)
        (Peter winces in pain.)
        (Then readjusts.)
alright then.
        (Pause.)
        (Take a breath.)
got that out of your system—?
        (Ray hits Peter again in the chest, harder.)

RAY.

…

PETER.

…

RAY.

…

PETER.
Ray!

>*(Ray punches Peter in the stomach.)*
>*(This one almost knocks Peter down.)*
>*(Peter takes a moment to recover.)*
>*(Then looks at Ray.)*
>*(Ray stares back.)*
>*(Then.)*
>*(Ray goes in for another hit, Peter pushes him back…)*
>*(Ray slips, falls, cracks his head on the tile.)*
>*(Ray's bleeding.)*
>*(Peter sees the blood.)*
>*(Peter approaches Ray.)*
>*(Ray lunges at Peter.)*
>*(Peter flails and fails to defend himself.)*
>*(Ray knocks Peter to the ground.)*
>*(Ray drags Peter to the edge of the pool.)*
>*(Ray dunks Peter's head under the water.)*
>*(For a count of 1)*
>*(2)*
>*(3)*
>*(4)*
>*(5)*
>*(6)*
>*(7)*

(8... Peter is struggling, squirming around, tries to—)

(9)

(10)

(11)

(12)

(13)

(14)

(15)

(16)

(17)

(Peter squirms again, but now the arms are starting to go limp.)

(18)

(19)

(Ray lets go.)

(Drags Peter out of the water.)

(Peter gasps for air.)

(Huge gasps of air, catching his breath.)

(Catching.)

(Catching his breath.)

(And catching his breath...)

(Peter reaches out his arm.)

(Reaches out his arm towards Ray.)

(Hits Ray in the face.)

(Ray hits back.)

(And Peter hits back.)

(And Ray hits back.)

(And Peter hits back, and again.)

(And Ray...)

(And Ray hits Peter.)

(...)

(...)

(…)
(And then…)
(Peter hits Ray.)
(…)
(…)
(Ray just stares at Peter.)
(…)
(And Ray sorta kinda throws a sorta kinda punch that misses.)
(…)
(Peter pushes Ray.)
(And Ray just sits there.)
(Just sits there.)
(Ray doesn't—)
(Ray just pants.)
(And Peter pants.)
(And the two pant.)
(And the two rest.)
(And for a good long while they rest.)
(And bleed.)
(Yeah, they're bleeding a lot.)
(And time passes.)
(Time passes.)

RAY.
… I'm tired of winning.

PETER. *(Weakly.)*
I'm sorry. I'm so sorry

RAY.
yeah

PETER.
…

RAY.

...

(Ray and Peter lie on the stage.)
(Totally, completely, absolutely exhausted.)
(Blackout.)

End of Play

ALTERNATE FIGHT SEQUENCE

PETER.
You don't put my life on the line so you can fuck some cunt

RAY.
don't call her that

PETER.
she's a cunt, Ray, she's
>   *(Ray walks over to Peter.)*
don't like when I call her a cunt—?

RAY.
no

PETER.
sorry but she's a
>   *(Ray hits Peter in the stomach.)*
>   *(Peter winces in pain.)*
>   *(Then readjusts.)*
alright then.
>   *(Pause.)*
>   *(Take a breath.)*
got that out of your system—?
>   *(Ray hits Peter again in the chest, harder.)*
RAY.
…

PETER.
…

RAY.
…

PETER.
Ray!
>   *(Ray punches Peter in the stomach.)*
>   *(This one almost knocks Peter down.)*

(Peter takes a moment to recover.)
(Then looks at Ray.)
(Ray stares back.)
(Then.)
(Ray goes in for another hit, Peter pushes him back…)
(Ray slips, falls, cracks his head on the tile.)
(Ray's bleeding.)
(Peter sees the blood.)
(Peter approaches Ray.)
(Ray lunges at Peter.)
(Peter flails and fails to defend himself.)
(Ray knocks Peter to the ground.)
(Peter starts to crawl away.)
(Ray grabs Peter from behind.)
(Grabs him in a stranglehold.)
(From behind.)
(Cutting off his air for a count of 1)
(2)
(3)
(4)
(5)
(6)
(7)
(8… Peter is struggling, squirming around, tries to—)
(9)
(10)
(11)
(12)
(13)
(14)
(15)

(16)

(17)

(Peter squirms again, but now the arms are starting to go limp.)

(18)

(19)

(Ray lets go.)

(Peter collapses face forward.)

(Then gasps for air.)

(Huge gasps of air, catching his breath.)

(Catching.)

(Catching his breath.)

(And catching his breath…)

(Peter reaches out his arm.)

(Reaches out his arm towards Ray.)

(Hits Ray in the face.)

(Ray hits back.)

(And Peter hits back.)

(And Ray hits back.)

(And Peter hits back, and again.)

(And Ray…)

(And Ray hits Peter.)

(…)

(…)

(…)

(And then…)

(Peter hits Ray.)

(…)

(…)

(Ray just stares at Peter.)

(…)

(And Ray sorta kinda throws a sorta kinda punch that misses.)

(…)
(Peter pushes Ray.)
(And Ray just sits there.)
(Just sits there.)
(Ray doesn't—)
(Ray just pants.)
(And Peter pants.)
(And the two pant.)
(And the two rest.)
(And for a good long while they rest.)
(And bleed.)
(Yeah, they're bleeding a lot.)
(And time passes.)

PROPERTY LIST

Baggies of baby carrots
Stop watch
Engagement ring
Swimming duffel bag with vials of medicine
FedEx envelope
Red Speedo with tattoo print on back

SOUND EFFECTS

Air horn